Jim Metcalf
COLLECTED POEMS

Jim Metcalf
COLLECTED POEMS

By
JIM METCALF

Foreword by
PHIL JOHNSON

PELICAN PUBLISHING COMPANY
Gretna 2000

The word "Pelican" and the depiction of a pelican are trademarks of Pelican Publishing Company, Inc., and are registered in the U.S. Patent and Trademark Office.

Library of Congress Cataloging-in-Publication Data

Metcalf, Jim.
   [Works. 1999]
   Jim Metcalf : collected poems / by Jim Metcalf ; foreword by Phil Johnson.
     p.   cm.
   ISBN 1-56554-701-2 (alk. paper)
   I. Title.
PS3563.E817A17   1999
811'.54—dc21   99-34687
                                  CIP

PS3563
.E817
A17
2000

Printed in the United States of America

Published by Pelican Publishing Company, Inc.
1000 Burmaster Street, Gretna, Louisiana 70053

Contents

Foreword

"The Anchorman"

Skipping through fields of eggshell egos,
Where the promise of sudden fame goes, he goes.
Oblivious of whatever ties there be
That bind him to mediocrity.

Jim Metcalf dropped this on my desk one day and waited
while I read it. "Anybody I know?" I asked. And he
smiled that quiet smile he saved for friends and said,
"Several, I would imagine." *More like scores,* I thought,
and I tucked it into my desk drawer and have saved it to
this day. Only four lines, and yet they speak volumes
about television in America . . . then and now.

Jim Metcalf knew all about egos and anchormen. He
worked for perhaps the biggest ego in America—Lyndon
Johnson. Or, at least, he worked for one of Mr. Johnson's
television stations in Texas as news director and anchor,
having first been lured from network affiliate WOAI-TV
in San Antonio, to which he would later return. It was
during the election campaign of 1960 that he got a call
from the owner, Senator Lyndon Johnson himself.
Johnson was running for vice president on the Democrat
ticket with Senator John F. Kennedy. He called to com-
plain, and complain most profanely, about a story Jim
had run the night before about his opponent on the
Republican ticket, Henry Cabot Lodge. "I can't imagine
why you would run a story about my opponent on my
air," he said, expletives deleted. "Don't ever let that hap-
pen again."

"But Senator Johnson," said Jim, "surely you must have forgotten that FCC rules mandate that we must give equal time to both candidates for any political office. We did a story on your candidacy the night before. Last night we did an equal-time piece on Mr. Lodge." There followed a series of growls and epithets and the phone being hung up—loudly. A few short minutes later the phone rang again. Again, it was Lyndon Johnson. "Metcalf," he stormed, "you're right, we got to give equal time. But I'm warning you, Metcalf, don't give that son-of-a-b**** a split second more, you hear me . . . " and he slammed the receiver down once more.

Jim came to WWL-TV in 1966 from WOAI-TV, where he had starred in a top-rated late afternoon show and anchored the 10:00 P.M. news, escaping the wrath of Lyndon Johnson, who, three years earlier, had succeeded the slain John F. Kennedy, and was now president of the United States. He signed on as an anchorman and reporter, and excelled in both. When the vagaries of the ratings book, and his health, gave way about the same time, he was relieved as an anchorman, and, gradually, medical problems forced him to the sidelines as a reporter. By late 1969 he had developed a pronounced jaundice, indicating cirrhotic problems with his liver. By the time I took over the WWL-TV News Department as news director in 1970, he had been exiled to a lonely desk in the back of the newsroom, assigned to watching the network feed and editing cuts we could use on the 10:00 P.M. newscast.

He was the first "problem" I sought to correct when I entered the newsroom. He was down, despondent, depressed, his eyes yellow from the jaundice. I couldn't believe he was the same man who had written such good pieces a few years earlier.

"What are you going to do with me?" he asked, seemingly knowing what the answer would be.

But I surprised him. "I want you to go home," I said. "I want you to find a good doctor and tell him to make you well. I don't want to see you again until you're well and ready to go to work. We'll mail your checks to the house."

He was surprised—but still cynical. "So what if I do get well," he said. "What do I do then?"

"Anything you want to do," I replied. And I looked him right in the eye. I think he suspected that I meant it. And I did.

Three months later he came back to the newsroom, thinned down, eyes bright . . . he was a pro again. And like a good pro, he had doubts. "I see you've saved my old desk," he said, pointing to the back of the room.

"That's not yours anymore," I said. "We're moving you up here, closer to the action."

He tried hard not to react. "What will I be doing . . . what's my assignment?"

My answer shook him visibly. "Whatever you want it to be."

"What do you mean?"

"Just what I said . . . you tell me what you do best . . . what you want to do." It was what he had hoped for, but really didn't expect.

He smiled that big, Texas smile. "I'd like to do feature stories . . . I'm at home with that."

"Good," I said. "We'll do two, three a week . . . think you could do that?"

"Yeah," he said. "Yeah, I can do that." And he was, indeed, well again.

And thus began the second coming of Jim Metcalf—fit, able, well again, and happy, yet seeing the world in a different light. He was totally in command—of his feelings, his emotions, and of the words that came forth . . . sometimes slowly, almost painfully, when he had a point to make, and sometimes they came tumbling out, like melons from a broken wagon, when he was happy and had to hurry to get it all on paper.

The Scrapbook came first . . . *Jim Metcalf's Scrapbook*, we called it, with a proper graphic to go with the title. He wrote essays, like Andy Rooney used to write for Harry Reasoner at CBS, pieces on windows, on doors, on mirrors . . . asking, and sometimes answering, the questions—who and what are on the other side? People reacted . . . they loved it. He was back in stride. And we found out that, when he was at his best, there were few in the business who could match him.

So Mike Early, the WWL-TV general manager, broached the inevitable—he gave Jim his own show, prime time, 9:30 P.M., on Sunday nights. It was madness. And the history of the medium in New Orleans was against it. Nobody, no *one* man, could ever carry a half-hour alone, especially on Sunday nights. So we hedged a little. The show would begin with a recap of the week's news, showing the old footage, beginning with Monday. And then Jim would work in notebook-like pieces. You got it . . . it was a bomb, proving for (I hope) the last time the old maxim that there is nothing staler than old news.

Jim, of course, had a better idea. "Give me the whole half-hour," he said. "I can do it . . . I know I can do it." Mike Early was never a man to let talent go begging. "You got it," he said. And thus was born *Jim Metcalf's Journal.* It was a masterful mix of pondering and satire, of true poetry, and dalliances like "The Anchorman." And there was spot where he would sit on a stool under a single spotlight. It was what he liked most of all, I think. It was pictures and music and, best of all, the words . . . those lovely, quixotic vowels spoken with that deep, resonant voice . . . that was part of the total picture, and the best part.

It was a magical decision. Jim's opening line, "Please, to begin . . . " became a New Orleans byword. He got requests for his opening theme. He beat the network shows running against him. And for one special show he won the Peabody Award, television's equivalent of the Pulitzer Prize. The years had been good. The poetry had touched hearts. His poems, collected within three volumes, were hot sellers—and he became the third best-selling poet in America. It was heady stuff. But he earned it. He deserved it.

And then, somehow, there was sensed in his poems a melancholy . . . winter had replaced spring, there was talk of parting . . . "parting is the price we pay for loving," he wrote. An again, in "Don't Pity Me My Years," he said, "I have lived and I have won/Life cannot cheat me now." And, from "Summer Lovers": "Love me now, and give me memories enough to last me through the lonely winter."

There was reason for the melancholy, for cold winter replacing the promises of spring. A medical check-up had uncovered a sarcoma . . . cancer—full-blown and terminal. Jim Metcalf died in March 1977, leaving these lines of tenderness and resignation: "I hope there is not time to say goodbye when my darkness comes/for I would not know how to bid my loves farewell . . . "

He is buried in a modest grave on the Mississippi's west bank, across the river from New Orleans, and in the shadow of the WWL-TV transmission tower. There is a tombstone bearing his name and a simple phrase . . . "Please, to begin . . . "

PHIL JOHNSON

Jim Metcalf
COLLECTED POEMS

Jim Metcalf's
Journal

Contents

The Poet and the Flowers

Once again we are betrayed,
the words and I . . .
faced with a challenge we cannot meet.
We cannot translate the quiet splendor
of a flower
into symbols set on paper . . .
or sounds the symbols signify.

We are impotent,
the words and I.
Inept, incapable,
awkward jesters of the court
mumbling through the sacred halls
    of beauty's majesty.

How could we presume
to describe the sweetness of a rose?
Colors heightened by the dew upon it,
    tears of happiness
shed upon its petals
when heaven saw the wonder
    it had made.

We admit defeat,
the words and I.
We cannot tell the story
of the flowers.
They do not need our counsel.
They have counsel with the angels.

Yet, if the last wondrous
bud should die,
and there would never be another
to replace it.
The angels would be as weak as we.
They could not find words to say farewell,
or music to sing a hymn
     in parting.
The angels could not say goodbye.
The angels would be weeping.

Togetherness

We walk where thousands walk
    among a sea of faces.
We hear the footsteps of those
who share with us
this time and place.
Yet, we walk alone and
    we are afraid.
For we cannot know what lives
behind the eyes that are reluctant
    to meet other eyes
in this gathering of strangers.
    We do not ask.
    We do not care.
Content we are to be left alone
in the throng.
To be passed by as we are passing . . .
unhurt, untouched,
save perhaps, the brushing of a shoulder
as we go our separate ways.
    Sing!
        A song of kindred souls.
    Hail!
        The brotherhood of man.

Obsession

If I am obsessed,
then let my affliction be
    a lust for beauty.
And let my search for it
    be in all places
and at all times.
And let it be
    never ending.

Help me to find it
where others have looked
and seen only ugliness.

In fields of weeds
    where wild winds
blow the vagrant sand,
show me some hidden desert flower,
    rich and full blooming . . .

A sprig of grass beneath
    the city's muddy snow
when Spring waits for the end
    of a malingering Winter.

Let me know
    the touch
of tiny hands . . .
    the scent
of summer mornings before the sun . . .
    the sounds
of laughter and muted organs
where stained glass windows are . . .
    the taste
of berries from vines
that cling to country fences.

And when the search leads me
to places that are barren,
    where no beauty is,
help me to create it.
To leave some sign
that there was one who passed
    and cared.

Flirtation

There was a time
when I could read the looks
on maidens' faces.
When I was young with roving heart,
I could see the faintest traces
of invitation
that flashed in eyes
that met my eyes.
And I could recognize
flirtation.

And I knew just what to do
to perpetuate the moment.
Knew how to smile
and be blasé.
Knew what putting on a show meant.

But somewhere between those days
and now,
I've lost my power to interpret.
And when I see a stray glance
come my way from some young
passing beauty,
I am frozen in dismay,
not knowing if I should look back . . .
Not knowing what to say . . .
without the slightest hint
of the intent
Behind the look she gives me.

Could be she finds the gray
that streaks my hair, suggests
worldly wisdom and maturity . . .
irresistible sophistication
and experienced impurity.

But I fear there is another possibility
and its consideration makes me sad.
Could be she looks at me that way
because I remind her of her dad.

Love

Of all the words in the language . . . "love" is, beyond a doubt, the most overworked, misused, most inclusive, talked about, written about, and perhaps most misunderstood. Ordinarily, the first thing that comes to mind when the word is mentioned is that ecstatic and mysterious relationship between boy and girl.

It can come, they say, at first sight or it can come slowly, as the two grow to know each other and decide they must be in love because they'd rather be together than apart. And sometimes they are right, it is indeed love. But as they grow older, they will find that the word means a lot of other things too—in fact, most things that are really worthwhile. They will find it is made up more of giving than of getting, more of helping than being helped, more of listening than of talking, more of seeing than being seen.

And they will find there is no such thing as loving a little bit; that it is pure and cannot be diluted, that it is total and only the total can be increased, strengthened, and broadened as their capacity to love increases. And whatever that capacity, it must be full at all stages of its development. And they will find it everywhere, this overworked word. In quiet places where the sun that streams through stained glass windows lights the faces of people, heads bowed in prayer. In hands that reach out to help and grasp a weaker hand, saying what no words can say. In eyes that sparkle still from wrinkled faces when friendly footsteps pad across antiseptic floors toward a bed that death is watching. In the voices of children as they clutch some tiny bit of fur that strayed from some unwanted litter, and the words, "Can I keep him please? I'll care for him . . . and I've already given him a name."

And they will find love in solitude. Sometime when the world is far away and nature's wonders are all about, there'll be sudden warmth and at the long day's dying they'll know they're not alone at all and that they will never be.

The Republic

Consider now, man's noble dream of freedom . . . this Republic . . . this America. If it should die suddenly one day, one day without the sounds of battle to signal its dying, if it were to slip away quietly in the sleep of our indifference, who would be the messengers of its defeat? And how would they tell the tale of a fallen colossus, and how it died, and why?

Would they say the dreams of those who gave it life were foolish and impractical? That those whose hands, in classic script, put ink to paper and fashioned words more fitting for the poet to ponder than for a nation to build its laws upon? Would they say young men of over half a dozen generations died for naught because they held those words near sacred? Or would they see that, imperfect though it was, it was not the framework that killed the nation . . . rather, it was the people; their apathy, their indifference, their taking it all for granted, like most things that were theirs, and assuming it would be forever . . . shaking their heads and shrugging when some symptom of an illness came to light and cried that it needed healing. The people, demanding with constant vigor the rights they were guaranteed, yet unwilling to claim responsibility for the ills that threatened that guarantee.

And perhaps, they would mention greed, these messengers of defeat. The greed of those in high places who would sell it all for a price, and the greed of the common man who demands his due while denying that of his neighbor.

It's a child, in years, as compared to other nations. A youth that leads the world. It is for us to nurture it, and not the other way. And if it should die of our neglect, the blood of the freedom that gave it life will stain our hands, and the clanging of the chains of bondage will echo from the mountain tops and through the desolate valleys of a barren land.

Class Reunion

The last paragraph of the letter read:

"And so Jim, we of the High School Homecoming Celebration Committee sincerely hope you can be with us and all your old classmates next month. As you know, this will be the first time we have ever attempted to get our graduating class together. It has been a long time since those wonderful pre-war years and we will, I am sure, have much to talk about."

Regards,
Dick Martin,Chairman

Dear Dick,
I regret that I will not be able to be with you for the homecoming celebration. I must be frank and tell you that it is neither the press of business nor the lack of time that precludes my being there. Rather it is fear. Fear that something very precious to me might be destroyed . . . the memories of those days, filled with the magnificent bewilderment of youth, when we were lean and eager, absurdly naive, summertime free and hopelessly in love with living.

I like to pretend that the people and the places are still there, just as they were when last I saw them. And sometimes, when it's important that I remember what being young was like, I go back in memory to those days.

If I were to see them now, the people and the places and the changes time has brought, my little game of make-believe would be over. It would fade into the world of reality that is, I believe, too much with us. There would be middle-aged people where children were supposed to be, fat where once there was muscle, and wrinkles would replace the dimples I recall on certain freckled faces.

And the places . . . the vacant lots . . . the gridirons of chilly Saturday afternoons in autumn, baseball diamonds under July's burning sun; they would not be vacant now, for progress would have grown in places that had felt the footsteps of our youth. And there would be plastic booths where tables with wrought iron legs and marble tops once held the sweet and wondrous delicacies from the soda fountain at Old Man Peters' drug store . . . and it would be air-conditioned. Gone would be the drone of wooden overhead fans that mingled with the talk of English Four, and who was going steady.

So if you will, Dick, give my regrets and tell all I'll be thinking of them. And when you hear them tell each other how they've changed, tell them that to me . . . they haven't . . . . .

Sincerely,
Jim

New Orleans

I turn away for just a little while,
then look back and you've grown some more.
The stone and steel of your towers
rising above your river
hold back the sunlight from the streets below.
Streets that wind and stretch and reach outward
to unintended places.
Through the swampland . . . into the forests and
beyond.
And the sounds of the city are heard
where only yesterday silence was.
What are the dimensions of this dream you follow?
How far will your cold and windowed columns
penetrate the sky?
What star to grasp?
What mountain top to gaze down upon?
And this web of asphalt and cement you weave . . .
these roads . . . these highways with obscure patterns
like cracked glaze on cheap dishes,
Where will they end?
What is their outer limit?
Follow your dream if you must.
But don't be obsessed with size
and growth.
Nor misled by the misconception
that giants are always strong.

Don't get too big, too soon.
And above all,
never forget what you really are . . .
this beautiful old enchantress . . .
this siren at the bend of the river . . .
this New Orleans.

The Time Between

I cannot recall when first I came to know
I was no longer young.
Suddenly, I was walking in the twilight
that glows between the years
of youth and those when we are old.
And now I find this wondrous world of
in between
holds the better parts of both.

I see loveliness and beauty
I had not the time to see before,
when youth's desires,
immediate and demanding,
blinded me to everything,
save the fever of the moment.

This twilight is the perfect time.
Would that I could hold it always.
But I fear that someday soon,
perhaps as I lay sleeping
in the darkness of these fleeting days,
my years will come upon me.
And when I awake
I will be old
and with uncertain hands that tremble,
I will grasp a cane to lean upon.

And I will see the beauty
that surrounds me now
through faded eyes.
And the colors of the sky
and all that lies beneath it
will be faded too.

So I will drink deeply of life's wine
while there is time to taste it.
And I will drink as much as I can hold.
And when it's over,
I will turn down
   an empty glass.

The Prisoner

My soul could write a million poems
if it were but free.
Compose a million symphonies . . .
Paint canvases to line the walls
of all the galleries in the world . . .
If it were but free.
But it is not.
It is the slave of me.
And though it begs to be released
and create its wondrous things,
I am an unrelenting master.
I draw the drapes of ugliness
That hold back the light
from the windows of my soul.
I let the chains of adverse circumstance
lock the doorways that lead to freedom.
And when the vagrant winds of discontent
blow chill within me
I resent the capability
of my prisoner.
And wish that it were strong enough
to break its bonds—
to free itself—
and make of me the slave.

Wanderer

I do not know what voice it is that calls to me
and beckons me to follow.
I do not know whence it comes, or why.
I know only that it makes within me
a restlessness
that compels me to go on searching,
as I have searched through all my years.

I have followed trails of steel
that cross the meadows and the marshes
and the mountains.
And I have seen the faces of those
along the way,
peering through doors
half open . . .
through windows
without curtains.

I have roamed the silent, tranquil skies
close to where the stars are.
I have outrun sunsets.
I have looked down
on eagles flying.
And watched the carefree, cotton clouds
meet with others of their kind,
convene, turn darker and then conspire
to mold a tempest,
and frighten lovers,
playing in the sun.

With swollen sails above my head
I have bowed to the will
of wayward winds
and touched the face of oceans.

I have found uncharted, secret isles
that no one knows but me.
And I have walked alone
along their shores.

But the voice that calls
and echoes through my days and nights
eludes me still.
And I must go on searching.
I have not the time to rest.

Seasons

The seasons are my undoing.
They make of me a fickle lover.
I see Autumn's face
in every face I see.
And I am overcome.
I cannot recall the look of Spring
that held my fancy
in the soft kiss of a quiet rain
last April.
All that was put aside
when first I felt the sweet, fresh
breath of Fall,
my latest love,
yet, most likely, not my last.
For it is the way of vagrant hearts
to trade one enchantment for another;
to hold one for a little while
before the search begins
for one that will replace it.
But for now, I will let Autumn's
charms caress me,
Before December's snows will part us.
Then I'll forget her face
as I forgot the face of April
when first I felt October's kiss.

Reincarnation

I do not want to live again
without the loves that I have known.
I do not want my soul
to be given to another
when by breath is stilled.
For whatever life might lie ahead
could not be half as wondrous
as the one I left behind.

For I have known the truths
that life is made of.
Known love,
have given and received it.
Known beauty,
and seen the face of God
reflected in it.

What more could I
look forward to?

They say I would not recall
that there was another time.
I do not believe it.
I think that, somehow,
I would always hear the songs
    of other violins
and smell the sweetness
    of other roses.

The Children

These fleeting moments
of your sunshine years,
these warm and golden seconds of your nights and days,
too soon will pass . . .
And leave you with half remembered moments
with no sequence.
Each a fading entity unto itself . . .
unrelated to any other.
Like shadows they will come and go;
the Christmas lights . . .
the birthday cakes . . .
the red balloons . . .
The brand new bikes
and popcorn from a paper bag
that dad held in the park one day.
Was it Spring?
Or was it Summer?
You will not recall
except that it was warm and nice
and that he laughed
and rode you on his shoulders.

If you could hold just one day of now
and remember it forever,
through all your dawns and dusks
and seasons giving way to seasons,
there would always be a part of you
the years could never change.
And though you might have seen
a hundred winters
there would be a certain look
of April in your eyes.

Interim Manifesto
(after graduation—before marriage)

This life I hold;
this life that is me,
is mine.
And I alone will live it.

Its patterns will be of my design.
Mine too, the dreams
that give it meaning.
And its loves
and hates
and all its other fevers.

This life is mine
to keep
or put aside.
The choice is mine.
And I alone will do the choosing.

For Not So Young Lovers

Youth has ended,
tomorrow we will be old.
Walk with me today
in the fading hours of this beautiful
in-between.
Hold my hand
and together we will go where we've never been
nor will e'er be again.
We will not dwell on what is gone
when youth's fever brought us each to each.
Nor on tomorrow's chilling winds of age.
We will set aside this day
to stand alone, independent of what has been
or will be.
Answerable not to calendars,
or clocks, or suns or moons
or tides that toll the knell of time.
And if it should be reported
sometime generations hence,
that a day is missing
from the charts men use to count the days,
we'll smile from some corner of eternity
and confess.
We took it, it was ours,
that day when spring was all about
and April begged to come inside.
We took it.
You can never have it back again.

Secrets

I do not ask why,
when suddenly in your eyes
I see a certain look
that does not fit the setting we are in,
the place, the pattern of our conversation.
A haunting look, and soft and wistful.

I do not ask what brought it there.
Or what it means.
But I know it is not of my doing.
And I am no part of it.

I know you must be hearing music
I have not heard.
Or words, perhaps,
whispered in another place.
Or remembering a springtime dream that died
when summer ended.

I wonder but I do not ask.
Because to love is not to own.
And we love because of what we know,
one about the other.
And that is all we need;
All that is important.

There is a special, secret place
where part of us is kept.
We save tiny remnants
from the fabric of our lives
and store them there.
And they are not for sharing.
Not to be judged
for their merit
or their logic.
Not to be passed upon . . .
save by the keeper of the keys
who alone can open the door
to the place wherein they dwell . . .
save by the one who put them there.

So I will not ask why,
when I lose you for a moment;
when I see that look upon your face.

And I will not answer
if you should ask
when you see it
on mine.

Windows

The stories windows tell are told in silence.
Like pages from a book when you're alone.
No sound is needed to tell the tale.
Windows that, like picture frames, enclose
tiny segments of lives
and hold them for a second before the scene
changes to some other.
Some tell of warmth and love and happiness
that dwell on the other side.
The side no passerby can see.
Save for a fleeting moment before the drawing
of the drapes shuts out the light
that overcomes the sudden darkness of a winter evening.
There are stories of violence the windows tell.
Boarded now, they tell of tragedy
and of how suddenly it came.
And how unexpectedly.
And how it touched the lives
of all who knew.
There are stories of despair they tell.
The windows whose dirty glass
reflects the hopelessness of poverty
where tired feet in worn-out shoes
shuffle down streets filled with the rubbish
that remains after hope has gone.

And there are windows that tell of man's desire
to own that which he cannot afford to buy.
See them as they beckon and entice
and show the stuff a sparkling dream
is made of.

Are they true
these stories that the windows tell
or are they sometimes make-believe?
You'll never really know for sure,
unless you see them from the other side.

Lifestyle

I am less afraid of dying
than of living without my loves;
the nearness of my dear, sweet people;
the music of words that sing to me
and the words that music speaks;
and colors
and sweet smelling things;
the touch of certain hands
and the changing moods of skies
when seasons change;
the magnificent arrogance of roses;
the majesty of eagles flying.

If I should be left with none of these,
then death would be my consolation.
And if darkness should be
the end of all of it,
what difference would there be?
To trade one world of darkness for another?
More to be feared than dying
is having love and beauty all around
And being part of neither.

Requiem for a Leaf

The covenants of spring have been fulfilled.
The promises of April kept.
You have lived your promised days.
And now, in beauty you are dying.

You have known the warmth of friendly suns . . .
The sweet, soft kiss of rains in summer . . .
danced on the wings of sudden breezes
to the music of feathered minstrels.
Felt the nearness of clouds above your head
and heard whispers from the lips of lovers
in shadows, sun flecked, at your feet.

And suddenly, it's over.
And it was all so fast.
Yet, you have known of life
all that is worthwhile to know.
Known beauty, all that is important.

So now, in the rich and splendid colors
of the robe of death you wear,
release your grasp and go
in loveliness.

Cling not to what is gone.
For the splendor that adorns you now
will fade.
And leave a shrunken, ugly thing
waiting for a spring that will not come;
denying death its pledge of beauty
with your passing.

Sea

I have walked in silence along your shores.
Have watched the changing patterns
of your moods.
And heard the songs you sing
to accompany them.

In the still of midnights,
summer warm and star laden
I have seen you.
Seen your face move gently in the
slow and certain cadence
of the breath of sleep.

Then, after waking,
in drowsy half awareness,
toy with a reflection of the moon
and change its shape
like the distorted mirror in a fun house
where we used to go
on summer holidays.

I have heard the sounds your ships make
crawling through a fog that covers you.
Heard their whistles
and their bells
and the voices of their men
cursing their maker for their blindness;
praying to their maker for deliverance.

I have seen you in sudden summer rages,
gray with anger;
frothing and screaming
and ravaging the land
and all upon it.
Taking that to which you have
no rightful claim.

Then, as if remorseful,
I have seen you give freely
of your treasures.
Seen you fill the holds of fishing ships.
Seen the life's blood of a nation
taken from your depths;
transfused by the towers of steel
that rise above you.

And I have heard your music
when you caress the sandy beaches
of a certain, far off place . . .
A secret island place
that no one knows,
but you and me.

The Day the Toys Died

$\mathscr{I}t$ had been raining most of the long afternoon and she had been staring out the window at the gray shrouded landscape for easily an hour. The soft light from the lamp was reflected like a new and shiny penny in the copper colored halo that was her hair.

In her eyes there was a certain sadness I had never seen before. And there was hurt there . . . and confusion. She was lost in the subtle and bewildering twilight that separates the fantasies of babyhood and the realities of adolescence. She was filling a cardboard box with toys that only yesterday had been so very real; so splendidly talented with versatility enough to play any role in the theatre of make-believe.

But, overnight, it seemed they had lost their powers and had become mere reminders of another time; a time that would never be again. She would, she said, give them to some little girl, now that she'd outgrown them.

She had packed them all away, save for a strange and faded little creature. We never knew just what it was. Some said it was a rabbit; others a kangaroo . . . a bear. But it really didn't matter. It was the object of her deepest love and together they had supped and slept. And walked and talked, and there was seldom one without the other.

She held it at arms length now, looking squarely into its face. Then suddenly she pulled it close to her, the way she used to when she was lonely or in trouble. She whispered something. I could not hear what. I was not supposed to. Then in sudden sweeping motion, she put it in the box and closed the flap and quietly left the room. She made no sound when she passed by me, but I could feel her crying.

And now she knew much of what life is made of. That there cannot be love without pain and the things we love are merely borrowed. And that one day, in one way or another, we will lose them.

And now she was aware that there cannot be growth without sacrifice and that there is no guarantee that what will come tomorrow will be half as precious as what was ours just yesterday.

Parenthood

The main trouble with being a parent is that you can't learn how to be one until you already are . . . if, in fact, you can learn at all.

There is a certain amount of preparation that can be done beforehand . . . you can read a lot about parenthood . . . you can talk with other people who are parents . . . but that's sort of like reading a book on flying and talking with a pilot, then jumping into a plane all alone and taking off.

And besides, the baby hasn't read the recommended literature or talked the situation over with anybody, so he's going to play the game as he sees it . . . ad lib all the way.

And if you have more than one, you have no doubt found that what worked for one will not necessarily work for another . . . . So what it boils down to is that you are one parent . . . or three . . . or four . . . depending on the number of children you have . . . one likes peanut butter . . . another prefers cold chili. It's hard to set down guidelines that all your progeny will even understand . . . much less follow.

And there is a point where the whole thing becomes academic. A point where they're not listening to anything you say anyway.

And it's then you realize you have raised a child . . . that your tutoring years are over, as far as he's concerned.

Now it's just a matter of hoping and waiting to see how it all turns out.

And if you see that you've made a mistake or two along the way, you might be given a second chance and you can tell your children how to raise their children . . . but don't bet your social security check they'll be listening . . . .

Auto Junkyard

Behold the cadavers left behind
by a civilization on the move.
Rusting relics that tell of
the restlessness of man.
Of how he runs and how motion
is more important than direction.

And when that which had propelled him
in his flight, failed
somewhere along the way,
when there was no life left in it,
he paused only long enough
to grab another painted carriage
on the passing carrousel
and set out on his way again.

And on his journey,
He will pass the same point many times.
And the beginnings
And the endings
will become as one.
A melding of infinities.

And these skeletons of steel
he leaves behind,
these hulls he brands as worthless
because they no longer move,
have a destiny fairer than his own.
For they will be reshaped . . . remolded
and made to live again.
What man can be certain
that he will?

Art

To leave behind some vestige of the thoughts we had . . .
the things we felt . . .
Some tangible evidence that proclaims us to be
more than things
that walked and breathed
and for a time occupied some tiny pace
in this universe.
This is the dream eternal of those who would create.
Those who would leave something of themselves . . .
something not here
before their coming.
A creation like no other . . .
as no man is like another.
And if it be beautiful to behold,
many will be the happier for it.
And if it is judged to be otherwise . . .
So be it.
If, in honesty it reflects
a thought . . .
a mood
or transient fantasy
of its creator,
art's purpose has been served.
The artist has had his say.
And perhaps, on some tomorrow
with changing circumstance,
there will be one to gaze upon it
and see beauty there.

Some someone
who understands.
Canvas, hung in half forgotten places . . .
Metal made red with heat
and molded . . .
Metal now grown cold . . .
Words that fade
on yellow, brittle paper . . .
These things and ten thousand others
say,
"I have lived.
I have felt.
And this I leave
as part of both."

A Farewell to Dreams

You can look back on them now and smile,
those dreams you vowed one day to own.
There were so many of them
and so few really worth the wanting.
Can you remember even half of them?
Or did they die and fade from mind
when a closer look killed the desire
that burned when seen from far away?

And the ones that did survive;
the dreams that stayed alive
through all the years
yet, were never to be fulfilled;
what of them, now that it's too late
to ever grasp them?

      They will die.
      They must.
But it's pointless to mourn their passing.
Think not so much of them,
as of all the good that came your way
without your even asking.
Perhaps these were the dreams of another,
of one who worked, yet saw them die.
They went to you instead
without your even trying.

Dwell not on what might have been
but on what has.
Be grateful for the road you've walked.
Forget the one not taken.

Judgment Day
(Circa 1900)

Withered Sunday afternoon ladies
after church,
around a quilting frame,
drinking milk
and eating cookies
and talking about Jesus
and Canaan land
And Jennifer Drummer.
     She's pregnant.
Could see it plain as day.
in church this morning,
underneath her choir robe
when she stood up straight.
She's showing, right enough and
     she's just fourteen.
     Just a child.
God'll punish her for sure.
A sinful child.
     And him too,
     whoever he is.
The Lord hates fornicators,
children or not.
Let us pray . . .
Lord, bless this food
and this drink
     to the nourishment
     of our bodies.
     Amen!
        Amen.

Crossroad

A parent to one who is no longer a child
and is leaving home for the first time

Soon now this path we've walked together . . .
the only one you've ever known,
will become two roads.
I will take the shorter one
that ends somewhere around a sudden turn
not far from here.
You will take the longer of the two.
The one that leads as far as you can see . . .
and beyond.
The one we all walk down alone
when life is young
and time is of no great consequence.
The road's the same for all of us.
But what we do along the way . . .
the byways we choose to take
or pass on by . . .
The stops we make
to consider some elusive, beckoning goal . . .
And those we meet
and choose to walk beside
and share what lies ahead . . .
These things make each journey
unlike any other.
And how do we part
now that the fork of the road
is in full view?
Do we say goodbye
and try to smile?

Then turn our backs
and walk away?
Then look back and wave
and take one final turn
and wait to hear the footsteps of the other
grow fainter . . .
And finally die away?
No . . . we will not do that at all.

You will take your road.
And you will walk away . . .
And look ahead . . .
And think ahead.
And I'll be here at the crossroads
until you disappear
over the horizon.
Then I'll take mine.
And it won't take long to reach the end,
so I'll walk ever so slowly.
And should you find
the meadows that line your way
less green than those you knew before . . .
Come back . . .
Call for me.
And I'll be close enough to hear.
And we will save the parting
for another day.

Bourbon Street at Dusk

Time to get up now, you tired old sinner.
You've been resting all day
behind those drapes you closed this morning,
just as the sun was coming up
and the day people were beginning to stir.

They're turning on your lights now,
so it's time to roll out . . .
cake on the make-up
and put those sparkling things in your hair . . .
those glittery things that attract
the convention guys.

Across the way, some of your friends
are taking battered old horns out of their cases.
A banjo's tuning up.
And somebody's fooling around with
an old upright piano.
Any minute now, they'll be bustin' loose
with a hand-me-down version of jazz.
Trying to hold onto the music
that all started somewhere around here . . .
somewhere, down around the river.
And you saw it all.

I guess you've seen about everything,
come to think of it.
Heard every sad story there is to tell,
and every bum joke.
Seen every stripper and every con man,
felt the bare feet of kids with long hair,
searching for something.
(God only knows what.)
You've heard the steady step of reformers
chasing sinners, drinking booze
from plastic cups.

That's your bag, old girl.
That's where you're at . . .
this is "New Orleens," as the tourists say,
and you're the star of the show.
Curtain's going up.
So, please to begin,
you lovable old phony.
You're not half as tough as you pretend.
I know.
I've seen you crying
when you thought no one was watching.

In Some Quiet Place

Contents

Some Tomorrow's Morning

On some tomorrow's morning
with sun fair rising,
dawn's pink and yellow fingers
will brush away
the secrets of the night . . .
the mysteries of darkness . . .
    leaving only truth to see,
    the substance of reality.

And I will understand
the meaning of my being,
the me of my existence
and what I am
and why,
    and what I am not
    but ought to be.
And the time of blindness
will be over,
on some tomorrow's morning.
    And I am uncertain.
    I am afraid . . .
Not sure that I can stand
the glare.
Perhaps, I need the darkness
to hide me from the truth!
    to keep me warm and safe
    'neath the blanket
    of my illusions.

The Cookout

The funeral was over, the Missouri skies were gray. The cold wind that swept across the small cemetery was scattering tiny snowflakes. They were banding together now, forming little glaciers in the rough dirt mound that rose above the place where she was buried. She had lived an incredible life, this woman, who as a widow raised a boy and a girl during the depths of the worst depression this nation has ever seen.

She had done alone what two parents often failed to do in those days, and she did it without ever asking for a handout. She did it through hard work, almost any kind she could get. Through determination, through love, and an unbelievable sense of humor . . . this woman who was our mother. She had a way of making good things out of bad ones, a gift that enabled her and us to see something ludicrous in the midst of the worst of crises.

One unbelievably gloomy day in December, when the temperature was below freezing, my sister and I came home from school and found her in an unusually happy frame of mind.

"Guess what we're going to do today?" she asked. "We're going outside and have a wiener roast. We'll gather some wood from the vacant lot next door, build a fire, and have a wiener roast."

We thought it strange with the weather as it was, but we didn't say so. After the fire had been built and the cooking done, we sat for a long time and talked, warmed by the fire and mugs of steaming coffee. When she was certain we were enjoying ourselves, she laughed and told us the real reason for the cookout. The utility company had disconnected our gas service because she couldn't pay the bill. The entire thing had been through necessity but she knew if she had told us, the cookout would have been no fun at all.

Her laugh was contagious and even after we had gone to bed for the night, an occasional giggle would echo through the quiet house as we contemplated her benign trickery.

We recalled that incident years later. The day of the funeral, my sister and I relived those few hours of our lives. When we got back to her house, the maid told us that the ice had broken the power lines . . . there was no electricity, no way to prepare dinner. Without saying a word, my sister went to the refrigerator, removed a package of wieners, and headed toward the glass doors that led to the patio.

"We're going to have a wiener roast," she said. "It's just the weather for it."

Our eyes met . . . and we smiled . . . for the first time in weeks . . . we smiled.

Waters of the River

My being
is as the waters of a river;
passing through time and change
and creations of God
and man
that line my way.
Ever changing, ever moving,
pursuing paths
not always of my choosing . . .
traveling at a pace
not always of my heart's desire,
toward some obscure horizon;
some uncertain destiny.

Like the river,
I am moved by powers
I cannot command;
sometimes to linger
in desolate and ugly places
'til I become
a part of what they are . . .
and their look
is on my face . . .
Then suddenly to be swept
past things of beauty,
things of worth,
too fast to grasp . . .
too fast to comprehend.

My life
is as the waters of a river
and I cannot change my course.

Perhaps, there was a time,
somewhere in the beginning,
but not now.
So I will take the path I must
toward whatever seas await me.

Twilight

And now, it dies . . .
this day that was ours
to shape,
to mould,
to make what we wanted it to be.
The darkness soon will steal it,
and it will be ours no more.

But in this death watch
of twilight,
behold, the majesty
of its passing,
and see the tapestry it weaves
and spreads out against the sky . . .
a farewell of gold
and blue on blue . . .
of orange and magenta.

And the rooftops of the city
pose against the backdrop
like actors on a stage,
competing with the grandeur
of the stage they play upon.

And the faceless silhouettes
of people
like shadows without names,
come and go,
oblivious, unseeing,
poorer by a day
than they were at dawn.

Before I Sleep

If I have let
this day pass by
and can't remember
something good about it,
then I have been ungrateful
     and I beg forgiveness.

If I have been involved
too much with me . . .
my wants and woes,
to see the beauty
that surrounds me,
then I have played the fool
     and I am sorry.

If I have not
stretched out my hands
to loved ones
to show them that I care,
then I have been unfeeling
     and I am ashamed.

If I have failed to help
when it was needed,
yet asked others to help me
then I have been selfish
     and I apologize.

If I have not seen
the face of God
reflected in a million ways
and places,
then I have been blind
        and I ask for another chance
to try again
            tomorrow.

A Thing of Beauty

I believe in beauty
for beauty's sake,
and that no matter
where it hides,
    it is never wasted.

If, in some dark
and secret place it lies,
where eyes of man
will never see it,
    it is no less lovely.

It needs neither praise
nor adoration
to justify its being.

It exists.
It need do no more
    to serve its purpose.

I believe in beauty
as a noble end
within itself.
And I believe
that God does.

Were it made
for man alone
it would not adorn
the silent floors of oceans
    where he will never walk.

Or be buried for eternity
beneath the sands
	of barren deserts.

If a man should wander
from his charted way
and chance upon
	a thing of beauty, hidden,
then it is he
who will be rewarded;
he who will be changed.

The thing of beauty
will remain the same.
As it was before he came,
so will it be
	when he is gone.

Mr. Amigo

She called me "Mr. Amigo." She was fourteen years old when I met her, one of nine children whose parents had come to this country from Mexico shortly after they were married. They had spent their days as migrant farm workers, traveling from one part of the country to another, harvesting the crops of the season. They worked in the fields . . . the parents and the children.

It was during the citrus harvest in the Rio Grande Valley of Texas that I met her—Alicia. She had not been well and was not strong enough to work in the fields, so she was selling newspapers to make her contribution to the family income.

On that first day she barged, unannounced, into my office and blurted, "Paper, friend?"

Already irritated by the fact that I had accomplished absolutely nothing that morning, I blurted back, without even looking up . . . "You can call me mister," I growled.

"Si," she said. "Mister . . . paper, Mister Friend . . . Mister Amigo?"

I looked at her face for the first time. She was smiling. I was stunned by her beauty; her face with eyes so dark, a magnificently delicate nose, and unbelievably white teeth behind her smile.

I shall remember that face always, as I shall remember her. For this child . . . this poorly educated, skinny little girl, changed my entire perspective and taught me much of truth and beauty and the simplicity of both.

She came by my office every day after that. I would buy

a paper and for whatever time I could spare, we talked. For every question I would ask, she had an answer, always simple but infinitely meaningful. Once I asked why she was always happy . . . happy smiling.

"Because I do things that make God happy," she said. "And when He is happy, He smiles at me and I smile back."

"How do you know what makes Him happy?" I asked.

"I just know," she said. "Everybody knows . . . He tells everybody but they do not always listen."

She talked often about her family and how they traveled from place to place. Once I asked her if they looked forward to a day when they could have a permanent home. She looked at me as though she could not believe the stupidity of the question. Almost indignantly she said, "We have a home now. We live always in each other's hearts and wherever we go, our home is with us. And as long as we are together, it will be so."

One day she walked into my office, and when I saw she was not smiling I knew the day I had dreaded had come. "We are leaving, Mr. Amigo. There is another place . . . another harvest."

Neither of us spoke for a long time. Finally, she leaned over my desk, kissed my cheek, and whispered, "Adios, Mr. Amigo . . . goodbye."

And she was gone. I knew I would never see her again.

Now, when I think back on all of it, I know I must have done something that made God very happy the day He sent her my way. And it was His smile I saw, reflected on Alicia's face.

The Search

I walk alone
in a quiet place.
Searching for the peace
I used to find there;
    but somehow,
        it eludes me.

The sun,
the sky,
the trees,
and the sweetness
of the silence
are all as I recall them.
Yet, there is a restlessness
    within me
        that was not there before.

And I cannot become a part
of the setting
I am in;
and the peace I seek
lies hidden;
perhaps beneath the rubble
    of some dream
        that crumbled,
or some tomb
    of disenchantment
        that took its place.

Perhaps, it no longer
lives at all.
Perhaps, it died
when youth did . . .
the day reality was born.

Other Years . . . Other Skies

(Circa 1971) . . . on seeing a flying
demonstration of World War II aircraft.

The years have been most kind to you,
my friends.
You've hardly changed at all
since last we met
at Uxbridge, outside London.
Or was it that old landing strip
between Liège and Brussels?
      Or maybe another one,
      after that,
in Fritzlar or in Aachen?
The dates, the times,
the sequences,
are not as easily recalled
as once they were;
but it's no matter.
I know we've met before.
I've seen you all
      at one time
      or another . . .
silhouetted against a contested sky
with death in metal capsules
spilling from your bellies,
      or waiting on ramps
      in foggy dawns
as lights came on in quonset huts
and young men awoke
from troubled sleep
and faced another day . . .

79

another nightmare
of reality . . .
then walked slowly to a briefing room
to find out where
it was to happen.
    And when they learned,
    they shrugged
and climbed aboard
and muttered,
"What the hell?
That's as good a place to die
as any."
Yes, I remember
all of you.
How could I forget?
We spent our youth together,
    and shared the dying
      of our innocence
    and the beginning
      of our fear.

The Gift of Love

I have heard men say
the greatest gift of all to give
is the gift of love.
I have heard,
but I do not understand.
I am not sure it is a gift;
a thing
to offer as a present.
I do not believe
there is the power within us
to choose . . . to decide
where our love will go;
to consider possibilities,
then make a list
and add names to it,
or cross them off,
and in the end proclaim:
"To these I will give my love . . .
to these my gift bequeath."

It cannot be so.
For if it were,
there would be no broken hearts,
no songs of love in vain.

It would be such a simple matter
when we received a gift of love,
to be fair
and give ours to the giver
in return;
if we had the power . . .
if we had the choice.

I think we do not give our love;
it is taken from us.
sometimes by those we want to have it,
by those whose love we've taken;
sometimes by those who take it
without knowing . . .
by those who do not care.

The ability to love
is the one true gift.
It is God's gift to all of us;
but He gives us not
the power
to dictate
where it goes.

The Door

When I walk alone
along the streets,
in unfamiliar places,
and see the doors
of houses that line my way,
I think of a house
I used to know,
and a door I lived behind.

A door that last I closed
    in anger,
      a long, long time ago.
And now, I can't remember why.

I only know I never did go back;
though I knew someone inside
    was crying.

I never did go back.
And now, it's too late to try.

A Dream I Overlooked

Now I will be going back;
back to where
my dreams began.

The day I turned,
looked back
and said goodbye,
and walked the path
that led to here
and now,
I thought I'd taken dreams enough
to last a hundred lifetimes.

But now I find that they are gone,
and I don't know where they went . . .
how many died . . .
how many spent . . .
how many realized . . .

I think I must have left
a few behind;
a few I overlooked.

Perhaps they may be there still . . .
somewhere,
in that quiet, untroubled place,
as bright and shiny new
as they were
when I first dreamed them.
So, I'll go back
and look,
and hope
I find just one
to hold
and keep alive,
in the brief and fleeting time
that I have left
for dreaming.

The Teacher

Walk slowly, little one
and let me walk beside you,
as you see the wonders
        you will see.
And I will try to see them
through your eyes . . .
eyes, still fresh
        and beauty seeking;
eyes that do not hide
behind the dimming veil
        of ugliness.

Tell me what you see
        when birds fly by . . .
        when buds of green appear
        on April's trees.
Tell me about the ripples
        on the pond,
        and the colors
        of the flowers.

There is so much
I need to know;
so much I have forgotten.
I remember only
        how to look.
I do not remember
        how to see.
So let me walk along with you
and share the world you know.
        I will be the learner.
        You will be the teacher.

Beauty in the Rain

If you fancy
that you have
an eye for beauty,
    test it
    on a rainy day . . .
A cold and foggy day
that wears no make-up.
    Test it
    in the shades of gray
that consume the sun
and rob the flowers
of their colors,
    leaving them forlorn
    in dingy places
like tired and aging ballerinas
in faded dancing clothes;
    huddling in the drafty wings
    of empty opera houses.

Gaze across the rooftops
and the chimneys,
painted
like Utrillo's Paris
on the canvas of the smoke
and fog
of a dying afternoon
in winter.

It takes
no eye for beauty
to find it
on a lovely day.
It thrusts itself upon you
        in the sunshine
        and the warm.

But it hides;
becomes aloof, elusive
        in the cold
        and in the rain.

The Island

In youth,
I dreamed of sailing ships
and voyages
to unknown places.

I dreamed I'd say farewell
to all I knew;
goodbye,
to things familiar.

Then I'd set out to sea
one day
and go where the winds
would blow me;
through storm and calm
and sun and starlight
dancing
on the midnight blue of oceans.

And the wind would sing
its songs to me
and tell me of
    a golden island,
where only peace and beauty were;
A place where I could spend my days
when I grew tired
of roaming.

But the dreams were only
dreams of youth,
and they, like youth,
have passed me.

And I know if there is
an isle of gold,
I need not travel far
to find it.
I know if it exists at all,
it is here . . .
somewhere within me.

My Final Sorrow

The wine of beauty
is all about me
and I cannot drink it all.
I must sip it
slowly
    from small and fragile cups.

For if I tried to have it
all at once
    (as is my first desire to do)
my senses would be dulled,
and I could not know
the magnificence
    of its bouquet.
So I must concentrate
on one majestic,
tiny world
that lives within
the larger one.

I must see the parts
alone
if I am to understand
the whole.
If a sunset I would follow
then the path of setting
I must pursue,
    forgetting that which lies
    outside the direction
        of my concern.

Yet, I know
if too long I spend
enthralled by a
single wonder,
I will not have time
to see them all
before the final darkness.

I will have spent my days . . .
and there will be
so much of beauty
I have missed . . .
so much I have not seen.
And this will be
my last regret.
This will be
my final sorrow.

If You Remember Me

I hope, if you remember me at all,
it will be for what I was,
not for what
you would have had me be,
or what others thought.

I hope that you will say
I knew much of love
and loving,
and dreaming dreams
that stayed alive
as long as I did.

I hope you will not say
that I was strong . . .
or weak . . .
without elaboration.

Say I was weak enough
to cry
when roses died;
to smile when others bloomed
to take their place.

Yet, strong enough
to be unashamed;
to admit
to being gentle.

Say I often walked my path alone
in winter's cold and barren places.
Say I played the loner's role,
but please add,
I was never lonely.

When Summer Dies

September has kissed
the face of a dying Summer,
and the chill winds of Fall
have come again,
breathing life
into a million half-dead memories . . .
    of smoke rising
from mounds of leaves
that fell from other trees
in other times
and places . . .
    of the wide Summer meadows
of youth,
and days of innocence
and laughter . . .
    of the warmth
of a certain lover's breath
in Winter,
beside a fire . . .
    of roads and crossroads
    and highways and byways
and people along the way.
And one memory begets another.
They come and go in flashes.

And all the times
and all the places . . .
all the feelings,
all the faces
you have ever known
  come back again
  when Summer dies.

The Agreement

They were young and they were in love and they wanted to be married. But there were religious differences and family involvements on both sides and they could see it would never work out . . . it would not be allowed to. So they agreed to see each other no more and they parted. After several weeks, the girl received a letter.

My dearest,
Let me tell you some of the things I have learned about being apart . . . some of the things you must avoid if we are to keep our agreement.

> Don't go to places we used to go.
> I did.
> It was dreadful.
> You'll find they are so much a part of both
> of us that they can never belong to one alone.
> Neither can they be shared with anyone else.
> They were not mine.
> They were not yours.
> They were ours, and they will always be.
> We cannot have them individually.
>
> Don't do any of the things we used to do.
> Forget the songs we listened to,
> the books we read aloud,
> the windows we looked through
> on rainy days,
> when the world outside was cold
> and we thanked God we had each other.

Forget holidays in the sun,
concerts on Sunday afternoons,
our poets' lines
and midnight wines
and bike trails
through September's red and yellow places.

Forget the breathless way
we threw ourselves at life.
Be sedate.
Be proper.
Change your style and change your hair
and be as far from what you are
as you can be.
And so will I.
And our love will die.
And we will too . . . inside,
but we will keep our bargain.

Winter Sleep

Our unfinished dreams of summer
were kept warm a while
by a kind but aging autumn.
But now,
they are still
and quiet
in a world that belongs to winter.

Gone is our lovely
red and amber season.
And the leaves
that shared with us
the secrets of a sunshine time,
run now before the wind.
    Hurrying, chasing,
    scurrying, racing
to oblivion.
And you are gone
and our dreams are cold.

But I think
they are still alive.
So I will pick them up
and take them back inside
and keep them
somewhere near the fire;
to sleep . . .
to wait along with me
'til April's at the door again . . .
  'til you
  and spring
  come back.

Sing a Song of Silence

Someday, when I can get away
to somewhere where silence is,
I'll while away
a golden day
listening in noiseless bliss.

For the first time in I don't know when
I'll open up my ears and let the quiet in.

I'll walk softly in some grassy place
and not make the faintest trace
of sound waves to vulgarize
my aural paradise.

I want no songs of birds,
no buzz of bees,
no sounds of waves on shore,
no breezes whispering through the trees,
just silence;
nothing more.

I've had enough of noise
to last a thousand lifetimes;
heard it every day
in every way
and throughout most my nighttimes.
Heard bangs and clangs
and screams and shouts . . .
heard booms and zooms
and swearing bouts
and whistles and sirens
and shootin' irons . . .

Some say the sudden silence
would set my mind awry.
Maybe . . .
maybe so . . .
but it's sure as hell worth a try.

A Place I Used to Go

There was a place
I used to go
when I was very young;
when there was no world
quite as real
as the world of books
and make-believe.

Across a meadow,
beneath the trees
that lined a sparkling stream
there was a magic land
where I was king
and others came
by invitation only.

Tom Sawyer used to drop around,
and Huck and Becky Thatcher.
And I remember
one time Tarzan came
and swam up and down the river.

Rupert Brooke and Robert Burns
would come and sit
and write poems
about wars and flowers.

But mostly, I was there alone,
watching the world around me;
and wondering things like
why the sky is blue
and how much a grain of sand
would weigh
if I were an ant.

I wish I could find
that land again;
but I've lost it,
somewhere, in the noise
and hurry.

And I wonder if Tom Sawyer
goes there still . . .
or if he grew old
like I did.

Parade

I look down upon the city
from a high
and silent place,
and watch the little people
walk the tiny streets.

I see them follow
one the other,
forming strange
and changing patterns.

And I wonder
if they know
what they are doing.
Do they have a reason why?

Or are they marching
to the sound
of madmen
beating drums
in hidden places?

Some Other Time Around

I think we must have loved
before.
Somewhere . . .
some other time around.
But I cannot recall
the setting
or the years.

I think the part I can remember . . .
the part
I'm calling now
is but a page . . .
a line or two, perhaps,
from a story that began
a long, long time ago;
when God was younger
and the world was newer
and we played other roles.

And when we turned to darkness,
when we no longer were,
the love we shared
somehow survived
and lived the centuries through.
Then we came back and claimed it
and thought that it was new.

We did not remember
that we had it for our own
before.

We did not know
it had grown stronger
while we were away.

I look at you
and wonder
what other times
we've shared.

I might have seen your face
through midnight fog
at Stonehenge.
Or seen the fires
when Rome burned,
reflected
in your eyes.

But I cannot recall.

I hope that if we meet again
ten thousand years from now,
I will remember
how you look tonight . . .
this moment . . .
just before
I kiss you.

Voices of the Bayous

In whispers quiet,
I hear the voices
from another time
echo through the bayous.
And I listen
to the tales they tell;
of life
and death . . .
of happiness
and sorrow . . .
of men
and boats
and sudden storms
and voyages unfinished.

Where are they now
whose dreams gave life
to wood and steel
and fashioned craft
to reap the harvest
of the water?

Where is he
who homeward came
at sunsets past
and waved to loved ones
waiting on the shore?
And where are they
who watched his face
as he drew near,
knowing the measure of the catch
would be reflected there?
I ask,
Where are they now?

And the voices whisper,
"They are here . . .
and will forever be . . .
in this quiet place . . .
here, beside the water . . . ."

Contents

Here and Hereafter

I do not dwell
on thoughts of hell
or heaven.
I love too much
this life . . .
this here and now
that God has given me.

I do not need the promise
of some perfect time hereafter
to explain away the questions;
the imperfections of today.

I do not need the threat
of fires eternal
to do whatever good is in me:
for that is born
of love . . .
not fear.

And its reward
is love returned;
not in some future life,
but now.

I do not know
how much more
God will give me,
or perhaps, take away.

I do not know
if this life is but a chapter
in a book . . .
or the book itself.

I know only
I will live it
as I will,
no matter
which is true.

Please
to Begi

Please
to Begin

Contents

Winter Visitor

If the time of April
were upon us,
you'd be just another day—
so much like the ones
that came before you
and the ones that would come after—
that your loveliness would go unnoticed
in the sameness of a springtime sequence,
when beauty follows beauty
from sun to moon to sun again.

But now, in winter,
you violate the mandates
of a calendar that dictates
what your nature ought to be . . .
and your warm kiss
is made the sweeter
when felt on cheeks
that recall the touch of winter . . .
just a day ago.

And the song you sing
of summer things,
reminds us
that the bleakest winter passes . . .
and that to sleep
is not to die.

Flock of Gulls

Swirl upward from the sea
like clouds of leaves
on anxious autumn winds
hurrying to erase
the final trace of summer.

Fly as free
as children's souls
are free . . .
as wide as the sea is wide.

Head out
to where the sea and sky
are one . . .
    and on the way,
     look back
and call a mourning call
for me . . .
a prisoner
with chains that bind me
to the shore.

Fog

Softly,
with a silken cutting edge,
the fog descends
and quietly decapitates
the towers that surround us.

Like Sleepy Hollow's headless ghost
they stand,
fading out of sight
into a limbo world
somewhere between earth and heaven.

And inside,
eyes through windows see
different versions of reality . . .
  depending on their point of view . . .
  the level of the window that they choose
  to look out and see it through.

Skyline

The dusk turns on the colored lights
and leaves the profile of the city
stuck against a pink and purple limbo
like black construction paper,
cut just so.
    Scissors with rounded points,
    little kids
    with little red tongues
    in mouth corners,
    cutting,
    gluing,
    crayolaing a poster:
"BEAUTIFY OUR CITY WEEK."
Regard the levels, children—
and the tiers
and the sudden jumps of man-made peaks.

Just the profile, please.
From a distance, please.
It's prettier that way . . .
    without the people showing.

Exodus

Another year is ending.
The pieces of the final days
are crumbling down.
Their hours and their minutes
melted
by the ceaseless tides of time,
they slip silently
    into the sea of memories
    that claims all our yesterdays.

And now,
in the impatient interim
between the wilting
of the Christmas tree
and the new year soon to be,
we wait . . .
    for endings
    and for beginnings.

But there will be neither.
Nothing will be changed,
save for a number.

The sun will rise and set
the same.
The winds will blow
and rivers flow,
    and seasons will give way to seasons
    as God will have them do.

And life will be
as it has always been—
    cycles within a circle,
    whirling
    without starts or finishes,
    through the timeless places
      of forever.

Clouds

The clouds,
like painted dreams of poets' souls,
roam the prairies of the sky.
They rise and fall
and billow and run,
free from the chains that bind us
to a world of limitations.

Yet,
they, too, have masters
that must be served.
They, too,
have their chains.
They go where they are told to go . . .
and when.

They can travel
no faster than the wind . . .
no higher than the air . . .
no lower than the sea.

Their freedom is, like ours,
a passing, sometimes thing—
a respite
now and then,
from the dictates of
a universe of law.

A Thank You Note on Father's Day for Marc, Michael, Jamie, and Clare

The gifts were lovely. I shall keep and cherish them forever—and I thank you for them. However, I have so much more to thank you for . . . gifts you have given me each day of your lives without ever knowing it.

I thank you for what you have made of me. For even with all my frailties and shortcomings, I would be much less a man without you.

You have made me stronger by putting me in situations that demanded strength, and though many times I wanted to turn my back and walk away, you would not let me. You looked to me in your helplessness and made me do what I had to do, and whether it was right or wrong, I acted, and grew stronger by it.

You have made me wiser by challenging my beliefs and causing me to question them. And some of them could not stand the test of closer scrutiny . . . the tracing of their origins . . . so they were discarded and with them went some hate . . . some prejudices I had not recognized as such before. And I am more tolerant without them.

You have made me less selfish. You have taught me how to WANT to give. Taught me that party dresses at a certain age are more important than three hundred dollar suits to impress a client. That footballs and baseballs and flutes and clarinets and college books and gasoline for klunkers are more important than savings bonds for retirement years.

I would never have believed all that before I came to know the four of you.

I thank you for showing me a kind of love I could not have known without you. And I grow cold when I think of all I would have missed.

My God . . . what I would have missed.

Sea Birds

Lonely,
and wondering
if you've gone for good,
I stood
and watched the sea birds
fly in before the sun today,
pulling summer
on a leash of cotton cloud
behind them.

One sweep they made
across the beach,
then back to sea again.

They've brought our lovely
bronze and azure season home.

Maybe they'll come back
tomorrow . . .
and maybe
they'll bring you.

Our Last Goodbye

Promise me
that when our time together
has been spent—
> *when we say our last goodbye—*
if you are left
to keep the memory
of what we felt
and what we were
and the beauty of our love,
> *you will not cry.*

For parting is the price
we pay for loving—
a pittance
> *for so wondrous a thing.*

Seasons bloom
and seasons die
and nights chase days
across the sky.
> *For every first hello*
> *there is a last goodbye.*

But for us,
the time between the two
has made it all worthwhile.
So remember
every precious day of it
    and don't cry,
      but smile.

Once in April

Once in April,
     running
through the meadows
of a timeless time,
I believed the promise
of a newborn season . . .
an eternity
of youth and spring.

Then in September,
     walking
in a quiet and wooded place
where trees stood
draped in sacrificial red and gold,
I felt the coming
of a somber season
and the sun was growing dim.

Now in December,
     sitting
by a fire,
I look out my window
at a barren land
I never saw before.

Where are the meadows
of that other time?
Where
the splendid shades of Autumn?

Somewhere,
across the way . . .
beyond the forest
still and gray,
another Spring lies sleeping,
waiting for its day.

But it will not be mine.
For my years now
belong to Winter.
    I've left my Aprils
    far behind.

Don't Pity Me My Years

I hope I don't see pity
in the young and eager eyes
I love,
when they look upon my face
someday
and see my years imprinted there—
 Wrinkles
they don't remember seeing
the last time that we met . . .

 A smile
that's not as ready,
not as quick . . .
 Eyes
that seem a little dimmer . . .
 A certain hesitation
when I speak.

Feel sadness,
if you must, my loves,
because our time together
soon will end.

But please don't pity me my years.
My beautiful,
my precious years . . .
my treasures every one . . .
my wealth . . .
my sustenance
for all the days to come.

No matter what the future holds,
how bleak the circumstance,
nothing can destroy
the joy
that I have known.

    I have lived
    and I have won.
    Life cannot cheat me now.

So, don't pity me my years,
my loves . . .
for I do not envy you
your youth.

Anniversary

The January day they were married
had been a cold, grey extension
of the night that came before it.
The sun had battled with the clouds—
had lost—
and now lay dying in a shroud of fog
above an invisible horizon.
And as they were walking
through the park,
the day became the night again,
and they never knew the difference.
They were in love,
and they made times and seasons
of their own.
They commanded suns and moons,
and it was warm or cold
or dawn or dusk,
as they would have it be.

But even with their powers,
they couldn't stop the years from passing.
And one day, they grew old.

Now, looking out a window
　　at young lovers,
　　laughing in the snow,
　　　they wonder
　　　how they keep so warm
　　　　in January's cold.

And I Will Meet Tomorrow

Across the way,
beyond the rooftops
and the trees,
the light surrenders wearily
to the darkness.
And quietly, another day is taken
from my allotted number.

Yet, the loss is made to seem
no loss at all
by the beauty
that surrounds its dying.
Wrapped in hues and colors,
not of death,
but brilliant shades of promise
and fulfillment . . . .
Pledges made in blue and gold
that there will be tomorrows,
clean, untouched . . .
as good or bad as I will have them be.

So I will not mourn
this day that dies at eventide.
I will let it take its place
with my other yesterdays.
And I will wait the darkness through,
and then
I will meet tomorrow.

The Library

Do the children still come here
as once we did
so long ago,
      to search,
      to dream,
      to find new worlds
they never knew existed?

Do they still fall in love
      with books?
Do they know
      their feel,
      their smell,
      their sound
when pages turn?
. . . like wind through autumn trees . . .

Have they shared
long winter afternoons
      and nights
      by hidden candlelight
      in quiet houses,
when all others were asleep?

Do they know of pirate ships
    with skull and crossbones
    flying . . .
    and stormy midnight
    horseback rides
to save the settlement
from dying?

And do they know
the craft men flew
    to reach the stars,
    long before the Astronauts
    were dreamed of?

All this we saw
    and heard,
    and felt,
in dimensions greater far
than moving shadows
    behind a pane of glass
    on an electronic improbability.

Do they still read . . . the children?
    Do they still
    know how?

Anchorman

Skipping through fields
of eggshell egos,
where the promise
of sudden fame goes,
he goes,
oblivious of whatever ties there be
that bind him to mediocrity.
Polishing the tools to carve his niche,
    (statements platitudinous,
    interpretations latitudinous)
all carefully intoned . . . falsetto rich.
With show biz cunning
and tutored wile,
covering ignorance
with a sexy smile.

Packaged in his hand—the world,
the ludicrous, the tragic,
shredded and baled
by electronic magic.

The king is on the throne.
The king is hailed.
(CUE THE KING!)

"Good evening . . .
17 ginglegarbs have cravvergasted
an oskolometer from the Frankensmuck
cornerstaff . . . More slakorbens after
this brief rennipuff."

In Parting

Goodbye,
sweet, gentle lover.
We shall not meet again.
The fever of our interlude
is over,
but we each have gained
a friend.
Goodbye,
sweet, gentle friend.
    May the songs you sing
    be happy ones . . .
    and the voices that you hear
    be filled with joy.
    May you walk through friendly meadows,
    flower bright
    and sunshine warm.
    May the hands of loved ones
    be close by
    to brush away the tears
    if you should cry.
      And someday,
        may you find the peace
            that only you
                can bring you.

Diary on the River

(Notes made while traveling from Natchez, Mississippi to New Orleans on the paddle-wheeler "Natchez" . . . Autumn of 1976)

It's noon now and the shoreline is still much as it has been since we left Natchez at dawn today . . . wild and undeveloped . . . like it must have been back in the 1800s, and I feel that maybe yesterday is hiding just around the bend and that I might pass right through it and never even know. There is nothing on either side to tell me what century I am in.

But suddenly, it is unmistakably today. Through a narrow clearing in the trees I see the sun reflected in the windshield of a speeding car, racing down some hidden highway. Above, a rope of white trails out behind a jet, unravels and stretches out of sight across the sky.

And yesterday is left behind . . . somewhere up the river.

But somehow, time doesn't seem as important when reckoned from the river. There is a sort of detached objectivity here.

A feeling that what is happening on the shores that line my way is not of my concern, for I am no part of it.

A feeling that I am merely an observer . . . impartial and uninvolved . . . passing through time and change, untouched by either . . . moving ever closer to the journey's end—the foreverness of the sea.

A Deeper Shade of Purple

The night is almost here.
There's room for just
one deeper shade of purple
to be spread between the layers
of the darkness and the light—
time for one last farewell glance
at the silhouette that was today.

How soon grown old . . .
How soon to die . . .
How little time
to find an antidote
for the ugliness it brought.

Yet, I cannot let it die this way.
Please let it show me
something beautiful
before it goes.

Not as much to please my senses
as to reassure my soul.

Suddenly, across the darkening way,
I see a field of yellow flowers sway.
White curtains on my window
flirt shamelessly
with a passing summer breeze,
and the sweet, sweet smell of clover
fills my room.

The lights in town are coming on
and up and down the street,
I hear mothers' voices
calling children home . . .
echoes from another time.

And now it ends.

The day has died in beauty.
My soul will be at peace.
And I will lay me down to rest . . .
And I will lay me down
to sleep.

Imperfections

Now it was ending . . .
this marriage that was,
like those who brought it into being,
so young . . . so very young.
It was dying in the afternoon
of a December day,
quietly,
in the cold of a harsh, unfeeling season.
And that day of sun and flowers
and bands of gold
and words, soft spoken
in a tiny chapel
when April was outside,
meant less than nothing now.

And they did not know
why it was happening as it was.
They could not say when or where
it started . . .
or how it grew
and led to this . . .
It just hadn't worked out
the way they thought it would,
they said.

It just hadn't worked out.
And there was no bitterness . . .
no hate . . .
It was, they said,
by mutual agreement.
They did not know
that each had expected too much—
That each had built a myth around
the other
and cast him in a role he could not play . . .
the role of a perfect human being.

And neither could accept the imperfections
of the other.

They did not know that imperfections
are what make love possible,
for without them, there would be nothing
to magnify those qualities
that might approach perfection.
There would be no room for change,
for growth.

They did not understand
that imperfections are people . . .
and life . . .
and the world.
And they are the challenges that
make living worthwhile.

And sometimes those who really love us,
love our imperfections most of all.

I know a little girl with freckles,
and she hates them.
But to me,
she would be plain
without them.

Lilacs and Rainy Days

It was over thirty years ago and it was Spring. The sudden roads of war machines lay muddy from the rains of early April and trailed like dingy scars across the face of Belgium's greenery; denying Spring its promise of new life, trampling newborn plants back into the ground before they had time to feel the sun.

It was a time when killing was in vogue, in a place where youth and innocence and beauty all were dying.

We were being moved from one someplace to another, riding on a truck, when suddenly I saw a little girl standing by the roadside. She was smiling the way little girls always smile when they have a secret they can hardly wait to tell. She was about eight, I guessed. Her feet were bare and her toes were digging little caves in the mud. There was a black lace scarf on her head and her face was the face of every child the world has ever known.

There was a small wicker basket at her side, and as we passed, she took sprigs of lilacs from it and threw them to us. I caught one . . . held it to my face and smelled it . . . then looked back and waved. She was smiling as she disappeared from view as we made a sudden turn.

She had said nothing. Yet, she had said much. With her flowers and her face, she had told us that somewhere things were still growing . . . that there was new life amidst the dying . . . that there were children still . . . and laughter and music and books and make-believe and loving . . . and being loved.

For all these years I have wondered where she went that day and if the war let her grow up, and if she is alive.

And I have wished that there were some way I could let her know that the scent of lilacs . . . and rainy days in Spring . . . will forever hold a very special place in the memory of one who shared them both with her for just a passing moment . . . so very long ago.

Sweet Retrospect

We choose the moments
and the days
we would like to live again . . .
forgetting those less pleasant ones
that came before—
and after.

And these hand-picked yesterdays
of our lives,
that we recall so fondly now,
are made to seem more precious
by the interval that lies between . . .
      sweeter than they were
      when they were today.
They were not so important then.
The present never seems to be.
      It is the present
        we take for granted.
      It is the past
        we glorify.

The Trees

They stood so proud—
the trees—
majestic creations
of some quiet miracle
that breathed life
into a barren land.

They gave freely
of their shade,
their timber,
and their fruit,
asking naught but that
a seed be buried for
some tomorrow's need.

Now, in defeat they lie,
felled by the tools
men use
in the name of progress.
   . . . PROGRESS . . .
That omnipotent euphemism
that confuses
advancement with change
and presumes
they are the same.

Summer Lovers

Let's hold our lovely, dying summer close
and share every minute that remains,
before the winds of autumn come,
leaping
from behind a sudden cloud.

For then, it will be goodbye.
    Goodbye to afternoons
    we cast in bronze,
    and barefoot trails
    across the sand.
    Goodbye to midnights,
    wading through the stars
    reflected on the water . . .
        to the changing patterns
        sea gulls make,
        and to crimson flowers,
        painted on the bay at dawn.

So love me now . . .
in this warm, together time.
Love me now . . .
and give me memories enough
to last me
through the lonely winter.

Soft Farewell

I hope there is not time
to say goodbye
when my darkness comes,
for I would not know how
to bid my loves farewell—
        or which to choose
        to share that final moment.

Which lips to kiss,
which hand to hold,
which sunset to recall,
which rose,
which song,
which season.

Please spare me the choosing.
        For I have loved so much of life—
        so much more than I have hated.

So many things,
so many ways,
so many times,
so many people.

Please let me see it
all as one
as I am leaving—
one single great adventure.

And let it embrace me
and take my breath
and close my eyes
and bid me
soft farewell.

Follow
Another Star

Contents

Dedicated to the Memory of
Jim Metcalf

"I have lived.
I have felt.
And this I leave
as part of both."

—*From* "Art," Jim Metcalf's Journal

Preface

As the poet himself might have begun: Herewith a note of explanation for the about to be read poems and commentaries of the late Jim Metcalf, who died believing what he lived and what he wrote.

It was with caution that I undertook the reading of the many pages of television scripts and the ultimate selection of Jim's heretofore unpublished works. The selection was made all the more difficult because of the knowledge that he had favored other selections for earlier publication through a uniquely objective system of self-criticism. However, it was in his nature never to reject entirely one of his writing progeny. Frequently he returned to major ideas in retired poems or commentaries to rewrite, refurbish, or combine thoughts, because he felt that what was good for one medium was, in some instances, inadequate for another. This, of course, cannot now be done.

The works appear exactly as they were written for television. It is my wish, as one who both loved and admired him, to retain all that was Jim in the works and then to pass them on to you, whom he believed to be a most unusual and select audience whether you be reading, listening, or viewing.

It is also my wish, as well as the wish of Jim's children— Marc, Michael, Jamie, and Clare—that you who read Jim's books will share with us a rich legacy of love, hope, and understanding and a nearness to the Creator of all things in the heavens and on the earth.

I sign myself . . . Mary Ann, wife of Jim Metcalf, an active title I so reluctantly relinquished at his death on March 8, 1977.

Some Distant Star

And what would have happened,
If on that day we set our sights
Upon a certain goal
And headed with determination toward it,
We had taken the other path
That seemed to beckon with almost equal promise . . .
The one that led the other way
And toward another, different life.

And do we now regret the choice . . .
Now that the choosing's over?
Perhaps there are those who do . . .
I am not one of them . . .
And do we think of what might have been
Had we walked along the road not taken?

To me that other way,
The way I might have gone,
Was too safe to offer challenge . . .
Too predictable to be exciting . . .
Designed to make of me a servant of another's deeds . . .
To display another's creativity . . .
To teach the thoughts of other men . . .
To speak their words . . . a parrot
Mouthing sounds to please a master . . .
Sounds without emotion.

And the goal I followed . . . still eludes me . . .
For I am not really certain what it is or if it is . . .
But the joys that came my way along the trails
That may one day lead me to it
Have made the journey worth the taking.
And if it were to end today,
It would still have been better far
Than the other way that might have lasted longer.

And should I find the light
From the distant star
I have pursued . . .
Is an illusion . . .
That it is but a lingering ray
From a rock in space
That has been dead ten million years . . .
If that light should fail
And tell me my dream was dead
Before I was born . . .
Then I will look above
For another light
And I will follow another star . . .
And I alone will choose the one to follow.

Look to the Rainbow

There was a rainbow in the sky early this morning,
Clearly visible from one end to the other.
I saw it from my porch as I went out to pick
   up the paper . . .
But if it had not been pointed out to me,
I probably would never even have noticed . . .
For I would not have been looking at the sky . . .
But downward at the paper,
Intent on finding out who had been killed
Or accused of something . . .
Or what building might have burned . . .
What train derailed or whether the golf tournament
   would be on TV . . .
And then suddenly it occurred to me that we don't
   look skyward much anymore . . .
Unless the weather is noisy or there's a jet plane
   screaming by . . .
We are in a sort of look around and down,
But not up syndrome.
I remembered how skywatching was once a way of life . . .
On warm, summer nights
Before there was TV or air conditioning . . .
And people used to sit outside and talk . . .
When families still had a lot to talk about and share,
The faces would inevitably turn upward toward the sky
To see the stars and the moon.

We'd talk about the Milky Way and how many light
    years away it was . . .
And how small man was in comparison to the Universe,
And how man would never set foot upon the moon
    because it just wasn't meant to be that way.
There would be no gravity to hold him down we
    thought . . .
And most certainly no air to breathe . . .
And besides it would take him a lifetime to get there,
Even if somebody could invent an airplane that would
    fly that high.
And we were content with that.
There were so many places on earth we hadn't seen . . .
Places like New York and Dallas and Rome and Paris
    and Istanbul . . .
We sort of felt that the Earth was ours
Because God had given it to us
And that the sky belonged to Him alone
And that somewhere way up there behind the stars,
He was watching us and all we did . . .
And there was a certain reverence in just
Looking up His way . . .
But all that got lost somewhere and it's hard now
To even find a place to watch the stars . . .
The street lights get in your eyes . . .
And the buildings in your way . . .
And sometimes the smog covers them.

And now that man has touched the moon,
Somehow it doesn't seem as magic
As it did when it was unattainable . . .
It was different in the hush of quiet summer evenings,
With the sound of familiar voices speaking softly . . .
The foreverness of the sky was all around . . .
In the face of beauty seen through
The fragile veil of childhood
And magnificent innocence.

As Others See Us

In a poem with the improbable and somewhat repugnant title, "To a Louse," the Scottish poet, Robert Burns, wrote the oft-quoted lines, "Oh would some power the giftie gie us, to see ourselves as ithers see us."

He was watching a louse as it crawled across the bonnet of a young woman who was sitting in front of him in church . . . and he deplored the fact that the little "crawlin' ferlie," as he called him, would have the audacity to assume so lofty a perch as the topmost towering height of the lady's bonnet . . . and it pained him to see that other members of the congregation were beginning to notice . . . and to point and smile, while the victim sat in utter oblivion . . . the epitome of a self-assured female . . . certain that she was being admired.

It was then that Burns formed the opinion that if we could see ourselves as others see us, it would free us of many a blunder and foolish notion . . . and perhaps it would . . . but it could also be psychologically devastating. Sometimes, for the general well-being of our egos, we are probably better off not knowing how we look to others. Take the lady with the louse on her bonnet for example . . . apparently she was never made aware of her predicament . . . and consequently left church, happy in her unawareness . . .

Consider now the anguish that would have resulted had she been able to see herself as others saw her . . . and imagine her complete frustration in trying to remain nonchalant while attempting to figure out how to get out of the situation and maintain some degree of dignity at the same time.

It would seem that we are better off the way things are . . . we don't know how we look to others . . . so we ask somebody. Now the trick here is never to ask somebody who will give us an objective opinion . . . no two people would agree anyway and we wouldn't know anymore than we did . . .

We should ask somebody who loves us. . .after all, they're the ones we're trying to please anyway . . . and they are going to tell us exactly what we want to hear . . . and by doing that, they the giftie gie us . . . to see ourselves as those who matter see us . . .

The Dream

Sometimes, in fitful sleep
There comes a dream
I have known from a hundred times before . . .
It weaves a fragile, mystic link
Between the things of long ago
And those of now . . .
And though I try to break that link,
And be once more a part of all that's gone . . .
I cannot . . .
I am and must remain an entity of both.

And the remembrances of things
As once I saw them . . .
Are faded by the blinding glare
That shows me what they are today.
I walk alone where once the crowds made noises,
As they watched youth in uniform
Compete for recognition . . .
And the sweat of eagerness
Stood on faces
Too young to be called men
And reflected the burning sun of August . . .
And the light of hero worship
That exploded victory was nigh.

I see familiar looking places
And remember the wondrous fragrance
Of apples and coffee fresh ground . . .
Men sitting around a fire
When the chill of winter was all about
And the fields that grew the crops were sleeping,
And waiting for the first warm touch of spring.
It almost looks the same . . .
But there are the plastic things to sell . . .
And somehow they don't belong.

I walk beside a carousel . . .
But I hear no music . . .
I touch the tiny horses . . .
And they do not move . . .
There is no laughter . . .
No tiny hands to reach for other bigger hands
In a moment of uncertainty.
This is not the way it was . . .
It was not this way at all . . .
There was the then and there is the now,
Each separate and distinct . . .
But the dream persists.
It weaves its bond between the two . . .
And I am left with only parts of each.

Preview

I played the fool for you, you know,
Last month when you dropped by;
With uncanny wile, with my heart in tow
You left me with a lie.

I knew you hadn't come to stay,
At least not for a while,
But I didn't think you'd go so far away,
So far that even your smile
Couldn't be seen through the winter clouds
That came when you left and hung like shrouds
Over the greenery
Your promise had given the scenery.

I took your picture in the park,
Welcomed you for all concerned,
And that very day before the dark,
You left . . . your bridges burned . . .
On Wednesday I wrote some words for you.
I labored, it was long and slow.
On Thursday, the sky took on a threatening hue.
On Friday we had a snow.

Now I see you're back again
But you won't break my heart asplinter.
It will be a long, long time my friend
Before I sing the last sad song of winter.

Oasis
(Circa 1974)

Behold the signs and logos
That tell of another time.
A time when the name was all important . . .
Ten billion gallons ago.

A time when we answered the question,
"How many please?"
Instead of asking,
"May I please have one or two, sir?"

And the only signs we look for now
Are signs of something going on.
Of people pulling in and pulling out,
With smiles upon their faces.

And meandering lines of those in waiting
Like dromedaries, slowly moving
Toward an oasis that promises fulfillment . . .
A flagon of the juice more precious
Than vintage wine,
The nectar rare that satisfies
The beast of burden's habit,
And though we see it, plain as day,
We are fearful we could be wrong
And that it's just a trick our vision plays
After we've been dry so long.
And we fear the oasis with all its promise
Will vanish as we come nigh,
And fade away . . . a mirage disappearing in the sky.

And we'll be stranded, although our pockets
Are lined with money . . .
The riches don't mean a thing at all,
'Cause cars don't run on milk and honey.

Attitudes

It is a fragile and wondrous fabric,
Woven of a mysterious thread . . .
This thing we hold and cling to
And defend instinctively
With no question as to why,
And we call it life . . .
And to each of us it has a different meaning.

For some, a great and magnificent journey
Where the hours of the days go by too fast
To savor all the joys that fill them.
For others, a long and arduous road
Where ugliness and self-inflicted misery
Lurk in all the undergrowth along the way,
And blind the traveler to the beauty that is
        everywhere,
Begging to be recognized.

Yet those who travel either path
Will fight death with equal vigor.
It is their common enemy,
No matter which road it intercepts.
Any life, they believe,
Is better than no life at all.
I do not agree.

The Impatient Interim

The time of the impatient interim is upon us.
The void of days that lies
Between the last, most splendid holiday
Of a year that's dying
And the first born of another.
And I wait . . . as a midwife waits . . .
With paper hat and cardboard horn and highballs
Near at hand
To assist in the delivery . . .
And I wait in limbo.
There is a thing, good and momentous,
That I plan to do.
But I will not waste it on the year that's ending.
I will save it for a new and shiny one
And put it in its record book
Before I've had the chance to add a blemish
That might more than offset it.
I think it is too late
To add it to this year's misadventures,
Too late to upgrade the average
Of successes versus failures,
So I will wait
And hibernate
And vegetate
And insulate
And isolate

'Til one second after midnight Tuesday . . .
Then I'll make my move
And score a point for good.
That will give me an early lead . . .
And with a little luck and perseverance
I might stay ahead,
At least 'til Wednesday.

The End of a Love Affair

Could it really be that the love affair is ending?
That the moment of parting is at hand?
That soon the bond we thought would last forever
Will be broken?
The love of the restless American . . .
For his wondrous traveling machine?

There is much talk about the break-up
And why it's turning out this way.
Surely not by the design or plans
Of either.
Rather, it would seem,
By some accident of circumstance.

Some say perhaps they had drunk too deeply
Of the cup that sustained their togetherness . . .
That the dregs are in the wine . . .
And there no vineyards are
To refill the casks,
Nor a billion years to await their aging.
The glass, once drained,
Can ne'er be filled again.

And others say one got the upper hand.
An imbalance in the whole affair.
A disagreement as to who owns whom
And who has the right to the lion's share
Of our precious, shrinking space . . .
And the smoke that rises from the embers
Of the dying love affair
Is all about us.
And in every corner of the city
We beg for the right to breathe.

You see, it wasn't love at all . . .
'Twas but infatuation with a servant . . .
A servant . . . and nothing more.
To be used only when the need arises . . .
And like a lover, 'tis more prudent to
Have but one . . .

Of Beliefs and Challenges

It inevitably comes as a shock when one of your beliefs is unexpectedly challenged and you are put in a position of defending it. When, in a moment devoid of emotion, a purely logical question is asked and you must justify something that has been a part of you for as long as you can remember . . . so long that you can't recall when and under what conditions you espoused it . . . and held it to be true and acted accordingly, without really thinking too much about the logic or lack of it involved.

And then, one day somebody asks the most devastating of all questions . . . "why?" . . . "Why do you believe this to be so?" You may or may not be able to come up with a satisfactory answer; and if you can't, then you begin to wonder and to question yourself and all your beliefs . . . and what you have based them on. After careful examination you might find that, in many instances, you really don't know . . . many from your religious background, of course . . . from educational background, certainly . . . but the others . . . those that just seem to come along . . . where do they come from? Through living . . . through people you have met and might not even remember . . . from dreams that died somewhere between youth and maturity . . . from suffering and seeing others suffer . . . from loving and being loved . . . from wars and the interludes of peace between . . . from the soft reassuring voice of a sweet lady as she held you on her apron-covered lap when your fever was high and there were no wonder drugs . . . These things and ten million more make us what we are and what we think . . . the moulders of our belief. And if they be other than logical, so be it. For happiness is not reserved only for those who have drunk deeply of logic's cold, demanding cup . . .

I'll Find You Again

I'll find you again
Someday . . .
When this here and now is over,
In a place we've
Never even dreamed of.

When this cycle
Of my nights and days
Is over,
I will sleep
Long, undreaming sleep.
And when I awake,
I'll start my search . . .
And I'll find you again.

I'll claim you
In the youth
Of some new existence,
Before there have been
Other promises
And old fears.

I'll look in fields
Where yellow flowers grow,
Remembering how you loved them so,
And on some hill
Where the wind blows free
And sets the flowers dancing,
I'll hear you
Call my name,
And I will turn and you'll be there,
And I'll hold you again.

Legacy of Love

What legacy will I leave for you . . .
What of me for you to keep
When I am no longer here to share . . .
What to leave that would be worth the claiming?
There will be no wealth as most men think of wealth . . .
No hoarded treasures gained as payment for my hours . . .
No jewels . . . or gold . . .
Or aging paper with numbers printed
And a signature that certifies its worth.
There will be none of these for this was not our way.
And I can but give to you . . .
That which you have given me . . .
That makes me worth remembering . . .
You gave me love.
I will leave you mine.
I think you would not ask for more
And I, I could not give you less.

Plants That Cling to Walls of Stone

Apart from others of their kind,
They cling to the only life they know . . .
Alone in improbable places . . .
Without the warm, sweet mother's touch of earth,
Were they orphaned by one of nature's capricious
    misadventures,
Or was it more?

Some miracle perhaps
That touched the cold and crumbling stone
And breathed life into a barren place . . .
And when that life was given,
When the miracle was over,
When the receivers of that life were left alone
To stand or fall,
What battles were fought to hold it
And who the adversaries?

How many midnight tempests have been conquered . . .
How many wayward winter winds . . .
How many suns of August's fever . . .
How many battles won . . .
How many yet to face before the final one . . .
The one that is inevitable?
And these lives that stood alone
And fought alone
Will end.

And who can say they would have chosen the other
Earthbound, sheltered life
Without a whisper of a challenge?
Who can say what choice,
If there had been a chance to do the choosing?

The Poet

In words that seemed created to go together
He fashioned music fit for angel voices.
At times fragile . . . delicate as gossamer . . .
And then in changing mood to fit a sudden passion,
They would explode like midnight thunder
Echoing through craggy canyons
In some desolate and silent land . . .

He wrote much about life and living,
For this was his obsession.
He held that most of us do not know what living is . . .
That life is made of little, seemingly unimportant
Minutes and seconds of our days,
And that we take them
And the people who share them with us for granted,
As we anticipate the fulfillment of
Some improbable miracle to change our lot . . .

And when he came home,
The people of the village implored him
To tell them where to find the happiness . . .
The beauty . . . the wondrous life he wrote about . . .
"What land," they asked, "what people?"
And he said . . .
"It is here . . . it is you . . . it is now . . .
Grasp it and hold it closely
For it is not forever."

But the people did not understand
And disappointed, they went their separate ways.
And that night, he who loved life the most
Because he had learned what living is,
Fell into a sudden sleep . . .
The Poet was dead.

Starlight

No matter
That you say
My star is dead.
That the light I've followed
All these years
Is but a fading afterglow
Of a world that burned awhile
Among the suns and moons,
Then threw its fire
Against the walls of Heaven,
Spent itself,
Grew cold
And died
Before I was even born.

It does not matter.

For it is the light
I follow,
Not the star.
It is the beauty,
Not the source.

Will not a rose bloom
Just as fair
When planted by gnarled hands?
Will not a hymn of praise
Played on a beggar's violin
Sound as sweet to God
As singing angel bands?

Gift of God

Near dawn,
Between the birth
And death
Of designated times,
There is a moment
God claims as His alone . . .
To prepare a gift
Of His design.
When He is done,
He bids the Sun
To burn the night away
And all around
The words rebound:
I give to you
Now this day!

Commentary on Morality

$\mathcal{A}$ person's concept of morality . . . of what is right and what is wrong . . . is largely an individual thing, frequently inconsistent and based more on a given situation than on an overall code covering a wide range of standards. But there seems to be a connection between the economic condition of a group and the general ideas of morality of those within that group. For example, during the Depression years, there was a common bond of understanding between most of the people in the country who had little, if any, money and practically no hope of acquiring any and who frequently lived their lives on a day-to-day basis, content with having a place to live and enough food to sustain themselves and their families. And out of this common understanding . . . this sharing of a seemingly never-ending problem, there came a great outpouring of kindness, of man helping man. A beggar asking for food was seldom turned away, if there was any food to give . . . hitchhikers traveled from one coast to the other in search of work, and catching a ride was no great problem . . . railroad men looked the other way while hobos boarded empty boxcars headed for somewhere . . . anywhere to earn a dollar.

But while they were being kind to each other, they wouldn't even question the morality of doing other things that were wrong . . . things they told themselves hurt nobody. Stealing electricity from the utility company, for example . . . the meters were simple in those days, and by inserting a U-shaped piece of copper wire in two holes in the bottom of it, the meter was bypassed and wouldn't move at all even if every appliance in the house was on and lights going full blast. These jumpers, as the U-shaped wires were called, were standard equipment in almost every household. As darkness approached, in went the jumpers . . . and if anybody had the slightest twinge of guilt about the matter, it certainly never showed.

Morality . . . who among us is to judge it? Who can pass judgment on a kindly old man who removed his jumper from the meter every morning before he left to open his grocery store a few blocks from his home. A tiny store that had the wondrous smell of apples and sawdust mingling with the smoke that came from the pipes of old men gathered around the stove . . . a store that sold a giant soup bone for a dime and left half a pound or so of meat on it, if your daddy was out of work.

Dear Enemies

You'd never know they are enemies
When you watch them strolling
Hand in hand
Or sitting for a little while,
Whispering words for no one else to hear,
But they are really in the midst of
The longest war in history . . .
The never-ending battle of the sexes.

Why, this apparent joy they are sharing now
Could be shattered in a moment
If he perchance suggested that
Women don't drive as well as men or
If she should suddenly smile and say,
"I can beat you playing golf."

The truce would terminate forthwith,
And each would charge into the battle zone
Flying flags of biological origin . . .
Each fighting for superiority
And for ammunition words
Like "chauvinist pig" and "women's libber."

But it is wise to avoid such confrontations
And let the truce linger as long as it will,
For we might as well admit one thing:
That while perfect we are not,
We are stuck with the undying certainty
That we're all each other's got.

Rault Fire
(November, 1972)

The panic of a brief period on a grey November after-
noon is over . . . an infinitesimal flash of time when
measured by whatever devices man uses to reckon eternity
by . . . a moment of life . . . death, and the agony
between . . .

What only yesterday morning stood as a proud mon-
ument to a dream, reaching skyward, white and gleam-
ing, has been humbled . . . burned and scarred, it bows
under a reluctant sun that shines weakly between the
passing clouds . . .

In the weeks and months to come there will be ques-
tions and some answers as to what happened and how
and what can be done to prevent such tragedies in the
future . . . but for today, the shattering reality is that it
did happen . . .

Those who died here . . . those they left to grieve and
those who looked on helplessly all have suffered . . . for
the dead, the moment of agony has passed . . . for their
loved ones, the numbness that came with the suddenness
of death will pass and, after the grieving, will gradually
come acceptance and the healing of the hurt . . .

For those in the streets below who looked on and wept and prayed . . . for those who tried in vain to help . . . for all of us, there must be solace that here in this tragedy we are shown again that beneath all the manifestations of hate, of misunderstanding and even of violence, there is a basic love of man for mankind . . . and a compelling sense of empathy in a time of great need . . .

And as long as this is true, even with all his imperfections and weaknesses . . . his frailties and frustrations . . . mankind will survive . . .

End of War

Eleven years and thirty-one days ago Tom Davis of Livingston, Tennessee, was killed on a narrow dusty road near Saigon . . . he was the first American soldier to die in Viet Nam . . .

In a nightmare of bullets and bombs and booby traps . . . amidst the loneliness and frustration of a war that couldn't be won . . . on battlefields with unpronounceable names, almost forty-six thousand men have been added to the list . . . another three hundred thousand men have been wounded . . .

Now, it appears that after Saturday these tragic lists will grow no more . . .

It seems inconceivable that these men, through their sacrifices, have not taught us something . . . something more than accepting peace as merely an interim arrangement between wars . . . more than agreements between nations . . . surely we must have learned that peace is people . . .

Peace is mankind advanced to his highest level . . . the pinnacle intended for him . . .

The question unanswered is have we advanced to that level? If we have not, then this period we enter now with such high hope is merely a part of a never-ending cycle, a war-no war syndrome . . .

And man will continue to kill man, in the name of some cause . . . and he will continue to talk of the immorality of war. And he will sign treaties and rest awhile, then kill again . . .

And he will remain much as he was when he first made known his presence on this earth . . .

City and Country Christmas

The city seethes and swarms
And rushes toward the final hour
And the people, as if preparing
For an alien invasion,
Run almost in panic,
Determined not to leave undone the things
They know they should have already done.
And the glitter and the tinsel
Light their way
And the blast of music,
Overamplified and distorted,
Jumps out of cheap loudspeakers,
Runs out into the streets
And joins the sounds of engines
And of wheels . . .
The cacophony of Christmas in the city!

It would be nice to get away
For just a little while, I think,
And get a different perspective
On the meaning of the season . . .
Somewhere in the country,
Beyond the buildings and the streets.
A place to wait quietly for Christmas day . . .
A place among the fields and meadows
Where man's decorations are not needed,
Where the browns and golds of winter
Blend with the evergreens and spread out
From country houses and wrap themselves
Around the tranquil land.

A place to prepare for Christmas
In a different kind of way.
Not by buying presents
Or decorating trees
Or singing carols
But by asking ourselves questions
About ourselves,
And what we believe
And if we really live accordingly.
A place where Christmas will come
Quietly . . . in splendor
And in dignity.

Time

What is it? This thing we call time . . .
There really isn't a good definition of it . . .
Probably the most widely accepted one is . . .
"The period during which something occurs."
But when you analyze that,
It really doesn't say much
Because the word period suggests the word time,
And you're right back where you started . . .
A period is a time and vice versa . . .
Anyway, whatever it is,
Man has devised a thousand ways to measure it . . .
And those devices are our masters.
We live by them whether we like it or not,
And they are everywhere . . .
In every shape, design, and disguise . . .
But make no mistake about it,
They are not on our side . . .
Some of them are beautiful . . .
But they are devious,
And even though many of them are guaranteed
Accurate to a fraction of a second,
All you have in the way of proof
Is the word of another device . . .
And the whole thing might be a conspiracy . . .
If you watch them closely,
You'll find they act pretty much as they please,
Depending on the situation.

They ring or buzz
Or clang you out of bed in the morning,
Then run at breakneck speed
'Til you're late to work.
Then for the next eight hours,
They dilly dally . . .
Snooze frequently and run only
When you look at them.
Then when the elongated work day is over,
They run like a bandit to catch up,
Throwing you late for dinner . . .
And we serve these masters without question,
When all the while they are measuring
The thing that makes us grow old . . .
And maybe that's the best definition of time.
Time is growing old . . .
And if you don't agree with that definition,
Then you're probably somewhere on
The lighter side of forty,
In which case, you can't speak
With any degree of authority on the subject.